For Every Girl

Amy Collins

Paranormal Crossroads & Publishing

For Every Girl

ISBN 978-0-9882412-5-1

www.paranormalcrossroads.com

Image copyright Amy Collins, 2012

Dedicated to:

James and Benny: Thank you so much for the love and support you both give! Thank you for encouraging me to write "from my heart."

My wonderful parents: Thank you so much for believing in me! I appreciate you always seeing the best in me.

My sisters: You are the two best friends anyone could ever have! I love you both!

Julie Hull: Thank you so much for encouraging me to continue writing "just 30 minutes every night", and also thank you for making my dream take flight!

Every Girl from Gravette Public Schools and Bentonville Public Schools: Always embrace the gifts you are given and use them to help others. Remember that you hold great value.

Contents

For Every Girl

Amy Collins

Forward

Faith, love, hopes, dreams, embarrassments, achievements, failures, success, heartaches, moments of great joy, disappointments, moments that take your breath away… These are the things that life is made of. Throughout your life, you will experience all of these, and how you react to them will make all the difference.

Many girls aspire to be a princess throughout their life. We want to be as they are portrayed in our favorite fairy tales: beautiful; liked by all; part of a great adventure; and the longing of true love. This includes me. Here is where being aware of how you see things comes in.

You are not given a choice of what you look like when you are born. You are not given the choice of the family, the culture, how much money your family has, or the talents or gifts you are given when you are born. However, you do have the choice of how you will react.

There was once a princess named Grace. Grace had many things happen in her life. Her father was a soldier and, sadly, was killed in combat. Her mother never really had time for her, and her step-dad was mean to her. Despite all of this, Grace made choices for her life. She was still kind to others, even though kindness was not being shown to her. She could have harbored, or held, a lot of anger in her heart for her situation, but she didn't. She could have felt sorry for herself and could have spent her life sad all of the time, but she didn't. Grace chose to focus on having joy and happiness in her life even when she faced hard times.

We are responsible for how we spend our lives. We can choose to live a life in which we feel good or not feel good. We choose our feelings. Now, before I go on, I do want every girl to understand… there are no bad feelings. They are what they are. However, you have a choice as to how much of one feeling you keep in your life. Constant or ongoing anger, resentment or sadness is not good for anyone. Does every girl at one time or another feel these? Yes! We all do. But putting all of our energy into those kinds of feelings does not make us feel very good, and people do not want to be around us if this is the energy we are putting out.

Let's go back to Grace. She chose a life of joy and happiness. Think of your happiest moment. How did you feel? How did others around you feel? Was your life different during your happiness? Most girls would answer yes to these questions. Why? Because joy and happiness make us feel good, and when we feel good others want to be around us because it makes them feel good as well.

This is why I am writing this book for girls. With everything that is out there today, we can easily lose sight of who we are and who we were created to be. Our lives are our own. We are responsible for writing our own history, and that history can be full of joy and happiness, or it can be a history full of anger and sadness.

This book is designed to help you refocus your thinking and it will go against the popular expectations of girls today. We will be focusing on these four topics: Beauty and Me; Friendship and Popularity; Your Great Adventure; and Love.

I am so glad that you chose to buy this book or that someone chose to buy it for you. I hope that by the end of this book, we will both have some tools to help guide us to a happily ever after.

Your Friend,

Amy Lynn Collins

CHAPTER ONE

Beauty and Me

Recipe for Beauty
1 Cup Optimism
½ Cup Truth
2 Cups Kindness
½ Cup Confidence

Mix all ingredients. Add a heaping handful of love,
a dash of mercy, and a tablespoon of humbleness.
Stir well and bake in joy and faith.

What is beauty? If I were to define beauty, I would say beauty is pleasing; to be beautiful; an outstanding example. Okay, so let's go over each of these.

First, pleasing. The first thing we need to notice is that every person on this planet has different things that please or delight their senses or their mind. What pleases or delights you? For me, beauty is a yellow rose, the smell of strawberries, seeing the sunset over the ocean, and watching the rain fall in a forest. This pleases me, and I delight in them. Look around you. There is beauty everywhere you look.

Second, to be beautiful. I think that this is the definition that gives us girls the most difficulty. We see in magazines and on television what a girl "should" look like. They are perfect looking: great hair, great facial features, skinny, no blemishes, perfect skin, perfect make-up…. I could go on and on. Most girls know that to get the images we see, there has been a lot of work done to those images. So, knowing this, what is our obsession with the "perfect look"?

No girl is just "ordinary." Each one of us was created out of love and made unique. If you look at the girls in your family, school or church you will find that there may be some girls that look similar to you, but they are not an exact copy of you. We are all unique. We all hold a special beauty, our own beauty. My beauty is not the same as yours, and your beauty is not the same as mine. Does that mean that I do not hold beauty, or that you do not hold beauty? No. It just means we are different.

This is one of my most favorite bible verses:

"You are altogether beautiful, my love; there is no flaw in you." ~Song of Solomon 4:7

God created each and every one of us. He made each of us unique. He is our heavenly Father and he tells us, "My daughter, you are beautiful. Everything about you is beautiful." Like most fathers, he uses a nickname for us, "my love." So he is saying, "My love, you are beautiful"! Wow! Really? Every girl desires to be called beautiful or for someone to even consider her beautiful. But notice the last part of the verse, "There is no flaw in you." I know what you are thinking because I think the same thing too, "But God, I don't have the perfect smile. I don't have the perfect face. I am not skinny. I have messy hair days." Did you notice that God did not say the verse like this, "You are beautiful, but…?" Many of you have probably heard your parents tell you that you are beautiful and you have probably told them, "You have to say that because you are my parent." I have said it or thought it. Parents love their children very much, but they are not going to lie to their children about matters of the heart, and desiring beauty is a matter of the heart. It is the essence, or center, of who girls are.

Third, an outstanding example. Okay, hold the phone. An outstanding example? Um, call me crazy, but have you heard this in any media sources lately? Beauty is an outstanding example? Okay, so maybe it is an outstanding example of what we are supposed to look like, but what about character? Do you ever hear anything about a woman or girl being beautiful because she is an outstanding example in character?

At the very beginning of this chapter, I chose "The Recipe for Beauty." Please reread this.

Seems simple enough right? I too am guilty of not always having the best character. It is very easy to find the bad points in others, but often more difficult to find the good. Something I have learned is that to be able to find the good in others, you must first get to know them. We have all done it. We have not hung out with a girl because the rumor is.... You can fill in the blank. How many times have we relied on rumors to make our decisions for us? Sadly, we have missed out on some really wonderful opportunities to make friends with new people.

How many times have we guarded our lips? I don't know about you, but I can probably open up a shoe store in my mouth because I have spoken unjustly, or unfairly, about someone or something. One flaw that many girls face is not thinking before they speak. I am just as guilty. How easy is this flaw to fix? All it takes is a make-over in using our brains first before we use our mouths. Silence can be a great thing. Telling someone to let you think about something before you share a thought is absolutely smart. Or, if you and some others are holding a conversation, just staying silent and thinking about the situation or whatever is being discussed is not bad.

My sisters are both brilliant women! They are both

accomplished, they have always been hard workers, and they are very good at articulating thoughts. They can think of things to say right off the bat. I, on the other hand, have always had to think about something before saying it. So needless to say, come-backs were usually thought of after the fact. For the longest time, I saw this as a flaw, especially at work because people need immediate answers. However, I have finally learned that there is nothing wrong with taking time to think before speaking.

When I do finally speak, I need to choose my words wisely. Are they spoken out of kindness? Are they with the intent of helping or encouraging someone? Am I focusing on the good?

My faith in God and faith in my family and friends reminds me of an important point. I am not ever alone. I have people in my life that support and love me, and I have a Heavenly Father that is by my side every hour of every day. You are not alone either. Who do you know that you can depend on… really depend on? Who do you know that will support and love you? On those days that you are not feeling so great about yourself, whom can you turn to for encouragement?

Do they have your best interest at heart? Do they support you positively? Do they encourage you positively? Moreover, do you do these things for your friends or family?

An outstanding example. I don't know about you, but this seems like a challenge to me. Most of us probably have the best of intentions and want only to do what's right, but we fall short from time to time. The word outstanding seems like a lot to live up to and may not be achievable if we make mistakes.

Being an outstanding example does not mean being perfect. Think of people in your life that you consider, or think of, as being an outstanding example. If you want another way of looking at it, who are your heroes? What is it about those people that you admire? What have you learned from them? Are they perfect all of the time? Have they made mistakes? You will find that yes, they too have made mistakes, but, again, the mistakes are not as important as the reaction to the mistakes.

To me, being an outstanding example is something that I want to strike for my life. I want to do good to others not so I can hear how wonderful I am, but because it is the right thing to do. Just as you have heroes, there is always someone looking to you and wanting you as their hero.

Beauty Activity:

1. In your own words, define beauty.

2. What do you see as beautiful?

3. What beauty do you find in yourself?

4. What beauty do you find in others?

5. What Bible verses can you find on beauty?

I'm Just Me

Whatever your style, don't change it! Love it! Love being the wonderful young woman God has created you to be!

What is wrong with girls just being who they are? Why do we think we must fit one type of style or mold? Why are we so afraid to say no to others' beliefs of how we should be? For some reason our society has us believing that we should all want the same things and look the same way.

Growing up, I never thought of myself as "special". I saw myself as just "plain old Amy". I wasn't popular in school, I didn't look like the girls in my grade, and I felt I had more flaws than anything. There were times that I was picked on because of my teeth, my high waist, the way I dressed, and so on. From that I felt that I could never measure up. There were times that I thought God had put me on Earth to be everyone else's joke.

I have a wonderful mom and dad, and I know it was just as hard for them as it was for me when I was in school, especially the junior high and high school years. It broke their hearts to see me hurt over the comments I would share with them. They were always there to encourage me and, of course, to them I was beautiful. The problem was, I didn't believe I was beautiful.

It wasn't until I went to college that I began to change my point of view of myself. People were more accepting and took the time to get to know me. I loved college! Not only were people treating me more like I was on the same level as them, but I was feeling better about myself too. My parents always had us in church, so it seemed only natural that I attend the Baptist Student Union in college. There I met many more friends and became part of a girls' Bible study. I felt during my college years that I grew closer to God. I applied more of his teachings to my life. And this is what I think changed my outlook on myself.

I was reading scriptures about how God loved me. I was able to talk with several other girls about feeling "just ordinary", and I learned I was not alone. Instead of wallowing in self pity, we were encouraging each other and pointing out the good qualities in each other.

I learned so much more about myself during my five years in college than I ever have. I learned I was stronger than I actually thought I was. I learned that I had much to contribute to others too. I began to see that I was special and that God had blessed me with different gifts to use not for me, but for others.

The one thing that I want every girl to know is that

YOU MATTER. You are beautiful, and you have so much to offer. Your story is different than mine, but no matter what obstacles you have faced, no matter what lies others have told you, you are precious and have been blessed with gifts to not only help you but to help others as well. Your gifts are not like mine or anyone else's. Your gifts are just as unique as you.

You have your own certain style. It may not be what society says it should be, and it may not be the same as mine. It is unique to you. You may be the one that never meets a stranger, the one that stands back and observes or the one who is always thinking of others. Whatever your style, don't change it! Love it! Love being the wonderful young woman God has created you to be! Instead of looking for all the things that are wrong with you, look for the things that are right with you. These things do not all have to be physical. No one else is like you. You are a jewel: precious, rare, and one of a kind. Love being "Just You"!

Just Me Activity:

1. What is your style?

2. What are your gifts? How can you use your gifts to help others?

3. What Bible verses can you find about personal gifts / talents?

Fads & Other Do Dads

You have to know your own style.

Fads and other do dads--geez. How much money have I spent in trying to keep up with different fads? From wearing the apparel of a famous singer or group to the purse that I carry, I have spent so much money.

I struggle with trying to be satisfied with what I have. I love jewelry, shoes and purses. I love seeing the latest fashions and trying to mimic them. I see people that I work with dressing a certain way or have a certain item that then entices me. So this section will definitely be speaking to me as well.

You have to know what you like and what you don't like. You have to know your own style before you start spending money, or believe me, you will be spending even more money because of bloopers on impulse buys.

You have to know your body, and what type of clothing fits you best. Just because you can't wear that cute dress that another girl can doesn't mean anything other than she is built differently. There are clothes that you are able to wear that she can't.

We tend to focus way too much at times on what we wear. Sometimes we allow ourselves to think that unless we wear the same clothes or have the same things as someone else, then we are no one. A Bible verse that I have to read often to redo my thinking is Matthew 6:28-34:

"And why do you worry about clothes? See how the lilies of the field grow. They do not labor or spin. Yet I tell you that not even Solomon in all his splendor was dressed like one of these. If that is how God clothes the grass of the field, which is here today and tomorrow is thrown into the fire, will he not much more clothe you, O you of little faith? So do not worry, saying, 'What shall we eat?' or 'What shall we drink?' or 'What shall we wear?' For the pagans run after all these things, and your heavenly Father knows that you need them. But seek first his kingdom and his righteousness, and all these things will be given to you as well. Therefore do not worry about tomorrow, for tomorrow will worry about itself. Each day has enough trouble of its own.

Again, normally this is not what society is teaching us. Society tells us that if we are not like this popular person or that one, then we are not beautiful or "in style," no pun intended.

What if society started focusing on our character instead of what we wore or how we looked? What changes would we see? Would we then begin to think of others more than we think of ourselves?

I know what it is like to want to fit in and to have what everyone else has. Believe me, I know. But should I really put all of my focus on those things? Is filling my closet and dresser with all of these do-dads really going to make me happier? Does this benefit or help anyone else? What will people really remember about me when I leave this earth, the clothes I wore the day before or the legacy I left behind? Which of these should be more important?

Legacy Activity:

1. What does "legacy" mean?

2. What is my legacy?

3. What are the important things I want people to remember about me?

4. What have I done to live out my legacy?

What's Inside

Beauty and fashion fade, but integrity and living a life with meaning linger.

The fashion industry is focused on one thing and one thing only… the outward appearance. Sadly, the fashion world has dictated to society how we should be, and our society has adopted this thought. We are to focus on the outward and ignore the inner appearance. Who cares if you are a giving, thoughtful person? As long as you look great, that is all that matters. This is the ideology we follow.

Think about your life. Think about your legacy. Beauty and fashion fade, but integrity and living your life with meaning linger. What do you do for others? How do you treat yourself?

We all have those nasty experiences that happen in our life. When they happen we tend to blame ourselves or feel that in some way we deserve this. Things happen in life. Bad things happen to good people at times. How we tend to handle those situations can make things better or worse. This includes our view of ourselves.

An activity that I learned during my master's program changed the way I think about myself and how

I treat my family. It is called "The Personal Bank Account."

Each of us has a personal bank account. Instead of focusing on money, our bank account focuses on the truths and lies we tell about ourselves. Just like a monetary (money) bank account, our personal bank account has deposits and withdrawals. This is how it works:

Anytime you say or think something negative about yourself, you are taking from your account (withdrawal). Anytime you say or think something positive about yourself, you are giving to your account (depositing). Just like in the monetary account, it is never good to be in the "red," which means that you are taking more than you have.

This way of thinking takes a change in our attitudes and how we think of ourselves. I have never heard a girl say, if she is being honest, that she just absolutely loves thinking badly about herself. None of us do. In fact, if all we are saying or thinking about ourselves is negative, it drains our spirit, which is who we are.

At the beginning of the book we talked about loving who you are and who you were created to be. Your thoughts play into this view of yourself. If you start making more deposits into your bank account, you will begin to see a change in your attitude and in how you feel about yourself. Here are some ideas of how to change your thinking:

1. Think about your accomplishments. The achievement does not have to be something big--maybe you held a door for someone or did a chore without being asked. What ever the accomplishment, celebrate it. Celebrate the small things!

2. Cheer for yourself. When you are getting ready in the morning, instead of focusing on the negative about yourself, point out the things you like about yourself. Cheer for just being you. We have to be our own cheerleaders and learn to love ourselves. No one else can bring us that confidence or love for ourselves, only we can do that.

3. Focus on Your Gifts. Each of us has gifts to offer to others. Think about your gifts and how you can use those gifts to help someone else.

4. Give to Others. This can be as easy or challenging as you want. Donate food to a shelter or food pantry. Donate your time to another child, maybe your brother or sister, and teach them something. Join a community service group and do projects to serve others in your community. Giving someone a smile is a charitable gift. If you do not have the money or the physical ability to give, you can simply give a smile. Giving to others helps us to appreciate ourselves more, and there is nothing more valuable than giving of yourself to help someone else, expect-

ing nothing in return.

If you focus on these things, I guarantee that you will feel happier and very pleased for being the unique person God created you to be.

Finding the Best of Me Activity:

1. What are 10 things you like about yourself? Write out your list.

2. Come up with a cheer to say to yourself. Say it to yourself each day.

3. What can you do to deposit to others' accounts?

The Garbage Man

Your past definitely impacts your present and your future, but it does not have to DETERMINE your present or your future.

We all have a history. In our history, we can think of good and bad. We can think of what we have done to or for others, and we can think about what others have done to or for us. What we carry inside of us comes out of us.

"The Garbage Man" is an activity that I learned about while in graduate school. The idea behind it is that you have a picture of a garbage man getting ready to carry off trash to throw in his truck, never to see the trash again. On the picture you can draw or write out the "trash" that you would like for him to carry away. Examples of the "trash" to be carried away could be: negative comments or actions people have made about you; negative comments or actions you have made to others; not forgiving someone; or judging someone before knowing them, just to name a few.

This is an activity that helps you deal with forgiveness and total acceptance of you. Accepting and loving yourself means being able to let go of hurts and losses. This is not an easy thing to do, but it is not impossible either.

CHAPTER TWO

Forgiveness

None of us are perfect. Learn from your mistakes and choose wiser in the future.

If there is one area that most people struggle with, it is forgiveness. It is so hard to let go of hurts and mistakes. Instead, we seek revenge or make ourselves feel awful for a mistake we have made. To us it seems that letting go is impossible... but, is it really?

Have you ever met a perfect person? I mean PER-FECT? Maybe someone you know and maybe even you strive to be perfect, but do they or you ever really reach that level? The answer is no. No one is perfect. We have all made mistakes. We have all hurt some-one at one time or another. We have all had someone hurt us. But does it help to hold onto the hurts and mistakes? What does your body tell you?

When I was younger and I knew I messed up, my

parents always had a consequence. To me, the person giving the hardest consequence was myself. I hated the thought of disappointing my parents. After they would sentence me with my punishment, I would go to my room and cry, and cry, and cry. During the crying I remember the negative self talk I gave myself, how "I was a loser," how "I was stupid," and on and on. Even after my parents and I talked and I apologized for my actions and they forgave me, it was always, and still is, so hard for me to let go of the mistake. My not letting go only hurt one person - me. I remember how I felt physically during those times. My stomach would feel like it was in knots, my shoulders sagged, my head would hang down in shame, I was sad or mad at myself, and overall I felt horrible.

Think now of things that you are holding onto. How do you feel physically holding onto those things? How do you feel emotionally? How are you talking to yourself? Who wants to spend life feeling revenge, hurt, or keeping track of all they or someone else did wrong? What kind of life is that? If we all answered honestly, none of us would want to live our lives this way. So how do we let go?

Forgiveness:

1. What things are you holding onto?

2. Write those things down and ask God to help you to forgive them.

Okay, So How?

If you are looking for ten steps of easy fixes to forgiveness, this is not the book. Forgiveness takes a lot from a person. It requires you to lay down your pride, let go of any anger or sadness, and move on.

PRIDE. We all have it, and it is not necessarily bad. If we were to define pride, we would find a meaning close to self-respect or valuing ourselves. These are positive. However, pride could also be defined as arrogance and conceit.

When someone does something or says something against us, our pride is the first thing that becomes hurt. We may see the action or words as a threat to our self-respect and value. However, when we start to get angry and have the negative thoughts towards that person, our pride takes another turn. It becomes us having a very high opinion of ourselves, not always a true opinion of who we are, and this part of our pride takes everything to a whole new level.

So to better explain this, here is an example. There is this game that I have learned about from the third and fourth graders at my school. At the lunch table, everyone is sitting around, and a question is asked of the group. The question is usually about an individual at the table, and it is usually to humiliate that individual. Let's say that John asks the group, "Who here at the table thinks Sally is horrible at soccer?" Then the group answers by putting their hand in the center of the table if they think this is true or keeping their hands in their lap if they think this is false. First of all, just like any of us, Sally is feeling embarrassed and hurt. Later on as she thinks about it more and more, anger starts to build up and she may be saying things to herself such as, "Who does John think he is? I am the best player on our team. They would be nowhere without me. Everyone goes to the game because of me." Okay, I know this is not the best of analogies but you get the point. She begins talking herself up to unbelievable heights. She may even say these things. Then out of her anger she starts to devise a plan to get revenge on John. Where is this all stemming from? Her PRIDE.

Does Sally have the right to be hurt and mad? Of course. Does she have the right to defend herself without hurting someone else? Absolutely. However, what a person says or does to us is the small part. How we handle it is everything. We can go down the road with John and do exactly the same thing back, or we can choose a different road. Now, taking the different road, many people think that is the "chicken" way out. But, ultimately, by reacting in anger to any situation, all you are doing is giving that person that hurt you MORE POWER.

There have been many times that I have been hurt

by others' words or actions. There are still things that I carry to this day that, just like you, I have to learn to let go. The people that hurt me have probably long forgotten the things they said and did to me. The only person still hanging onto them and giving them power is me.

So how do we let go of the negative side of pride and still value ourselves? How do we forgive even if someone never apologized or asked for forgiveness? What if we made a huge mistake, how could we ever forgive ourselves? Like I said earlier, none of us are perfect. As we get older, one thing remains the same - PEOPLE MAKE MISTAKES.

I think back to when I was in fourth grade. I knew what it was like to be teased. I knew how it felt to hear people say awful things about me, yet when an opportunity arose for me to stand up for someone, I stood back. There was a sweet girl in our class who didn't have a lot of friends. In fact she was more of a loner. Her family was poor, her clothes were not always clean, and she always smelled. Girls would tease her and ask if she had peed on herself. This was an everyday thing for this poor girl. I heard the remarks but never stood up for her, mainly out of fear for what the girls would do or start saying about me.

When Christmas came around, we had our class party. Everyone brought delicious treats to share. The sweet girl came to our party and she brought a treat for everyone: lima beans. As if the smelling jokes were not bad enough, now there was something else to tease her about. I remember being in the bathroom at the same time as her and a group of the "popular girls." They began teasing her about how she smelled and hoe she brought the lima beans. Again, I said nothing out of fear. As they teased and taunted her, the look on her face showed a sadness that I had never seen before. That sadness soon turned to anger and she would start to insult them, yell at them and do whatever she could to stand up for herself.

To this day, I still wonder what happened to this young lady. I wonder if she is living a good life, and, even though we had never asked her for forgiveness, I wonder if she was able to let go of those lies and move on. I wish to this day that I could apologize to her for not standing up for her.

I tell this story to point out that she had every reason to be upset. There was a lot of PRIDE going on. I let my pride get in the way because I was worried about my value and self-respect being teased. The girls doing the teasing and taunting were prideful. Although they may have been popular, they had faults too, but they let their pride get in the way of their better judgment.

LET GO OF THE ANGER AND SADNESS. The

one thing I am always telling students at my school is, "Remember, the person doing the teasing or taunting is the person that has the problem, NOT YOU." Do not let someone else's opinion of you define you. Be proud of yourself and value yourself, but never put yourself above anyone else. We are all human. We all make mistakes. We all have things in our past that we are not proud of. Lay down your pride.

As I said earlier, the people who have hurt you have probably moved on and never gave what they did to you a second thought. So why do we hold onto those hurts? Holding onto anger or sadness does not feel good, yet for some reason we keep them. I have been told by many students and adults that it is hard to let go of the sadness or anger. Ultimately, it is you who can control all of that.

Something that is useful is to write a letter to the person that hurt you. Describe in detail what it is that they did and how it made you feel. Tell all the feelings that you had. When you are done, you can either give it to the person or you can throw it away. The point is, you are trying to get it out of you.

MOVE ON.

Some other ways to help you forgive:

• Write on the outside of a balloon what the person has either said or done to you. Then blow the balloon up, tie the knot, and release the balloon into the air. This is a visual way of showing that you are letting the problem go. Once it is gone, it is gone. If you catch yourself thinking about it, think of the positive things happening in your life.

• One thing that truly helps me is reading Bible verses and quotes about forgiveness.

• Learn from your hurts. If someone has hurt you, learn from it. Learn to show kindness and tenderness to others.

• None of us are perfect. We all have had our moments of saying or doing things that we know we should not have done, but we must let it go. Learn from your mistakes and choose wiser in the future.

CHAPTER THREE

Friendship and Popularity

You are the world to your friend, and your friend is the world to you. Treat each other that way.

Friendships are one of the biggest blessings we can have in life. When you find someone that shares in the same interests and values as you, shares your differences, and shares life's ups and downs, that is someone you want to treasure. There are so many quotes and sayings about friendship. This is no accident. Friendships are one of the strongest relationships that anyone can have. However, like any relationship, friendship takes work. It takes you putting yourself on the back burner and putting someone else first, but it also takes you standing up for what you believe is right in some situations.

The one thing that I wish all girls would understand when it comes to friendship is that friends are not going to agree on EVERYTHING ALL THE TIME. You and your friends are different people. You are going to see things differently sometimes or you may like different things. Being different is absolutely okay. However, just because you have these differences does not mean you have to stop being friends. In fact, this is when friendships are really tested. You can both learn to respect one another even though you have differences.

For example, my really good friend Jeni does not like cheese. She cannot stand cheese. However, I love it! I could put it on anything! I am still her friend, and I respect her. I don't make her feel guilty or "weird" because she does not like cheese. Now, this is just one small example. She and I also stand on different positions on politics, religion, and some other parts of life, but we do not allow these differences to come between us. In fact, it is cool that we have different views because it allows us to "get out of our box" and learn to look at things from different perspectives. We don't give up where we stand, but we open our eyes to how the other person sees things.

I do a lesson with all of my classes called "Friends are a Jewel." I take in glass marbles, the ones you put in the bottom of fish tanks, and I give two "jewels" to each student in the class. I tell them that friends are jewels and they are precious and rare. One of the "jewels" represents the student and the other their best friend. We talk about how people treat jewels: protect them, clean them so they shine, show them off, etc. We then talk about how just as you would do these things for a jewel that you need to do them for your friend as well. To do that you would speak kindly to your friend, do nice things for them, stand up for them and when they have an accomplishment CELEBRATE with them.

Friends are here to help us through life's journey, and we are here to help them. Today do something unexpected for your friend. Let them know how special they are to you. You are the world to your friend and your friend is the world to you. Treat each other that way.

Friendship Activity:

1. List your friends and what you like about them.

2. Today do something unexpected for your friends.

3. What Bible verses can you find on friendship?

Look in the Mirror
if You Want Friends

What are you doing to be a friend to someone else?

Think about the people you call friends in your life. Why do you call them your friend? What about them do you admire? Then think about yourself. Why do others call you their friend? What about you do they admire?

Earlier we talked about knowing yourself. To truly know yourself you have to be able to point out your strengths and your weaknesses. You need to know where you stand on certain values. You need to know what you like. But, most importantly, you need to know the talents and gifts you have that you can share with others.

As I am writing this, I am thinking about the many girls in my life that I call friends. I am thinking about what makes each of them so special to me. We are all so different, and they have so many talents and gifts that I wish I could possess: several of them are so funny and know just when to tell that funny story or joke; several of them have thoughtfulness beyond measure, they remember even the small things; several of them go above and beyond helping. As I think about the qualities and talents they all have, I realize how wonderfully blessed I am to have these people in my life, and my only hope is that I am as good a friend to them as they are to me.

Again, think about your gifts. What do you have to offer to your friends? Think about the small things that you do for your friends. Believe me, the small things always mean more than the big things.

One of my favorite things to do for others is making cards. I love to use scrap booking materials to create my "work of art." I love looking through quotes to put inside of these creations to let someone know how much I love and appreciate them. I love trying to match up items that I think symbolize that person's personality. Even though they are not perfect, I feel this a gift I am giving to my friends and family.

Availability is the number one thing I appreciate in my friends. I have friends that I may not talk to every day, every week or every month, but I know that if I pick up that phone and call they will answer my call and be there if I need anything. I work really hard to be sure I am available to them as well.

Life is so full of obstacles and achievements. Our friends need us in helping them through the obstacles by offering good or wise advice or by sitting back, really paying attention and just listening to them.

On the flip side, they also need to know that if they have an achievement that we will be there to cheer them on and celebrate with them. Life is too short for jealousy, and too often we get jealous of someone else's achievement rather than celebrating this wonderful time in their life.

I titled this chapter for a very important reason. I hear girls say way too often, "I don't have any friends." My first question to them is "What are you doing to be a friend to someone else?" We cannot just go up to someone and expect them to automatically be our friend. Friendship takes time. You have to give of yourself without expecting anything in return. You have to be able to put yourself in someone else's shoes. You have to be able to appreciate others' differences. You have to be honest and dependable. So before you start with, "I don't have any friends," stop and think if you are being a friend.

Being a Friend Activity:

1. Define what a friend is.

2. How are you being a friend to others?

We're In A Fight and Now We're Friends Again

Friends may argue and fight, but if your friend is able to come to you with open arms and call you friend, they are a true friend.

From time to time you and your friend may get in a disagreement, or one of you may do something to the other that hurts their feelings. We are not perfect, and we are going to make mistakes.

I cannot tell you the amount of times I have heard girls complain about how they fight with each other and they think they may need to stop being friends. Disagreeing and feeling hurt are both parts of any relationship. A lot of the time our friends do not mean to hurt us, but we take it as them being mean to us and so we react defensively.

When talking with your friends, if you take something as hurtful tell your friend, "I didn't like it when…," or, "I felt hurt when…" Always start with "I". Starting with "you" makes it sound like you are already accusing your friend, which then makes them upset. Also, you need to be prepared if your friend shares a statement like the ones above with you. If you have done something, even if you did not mean it the way it came across, apologize.

One of the most important things to have in a friendship is forgiveness. Lay down your pride and apologize when you are wrong. Also remember that your friend is not perfect and forgive them when they apologize to you.

Sometimes, I tell girls to hang out with different friends. Sometimes just being with the same person all the time becomes too much. You start arguing and become annoying to each other. It is absolutely okay to have other friends and hang out with them. However, never treat any of your friends badly. Do not gossip about them, do not leave them out, and always come back and spend time with them.

You are going to have some difficult times in your friendship. Be patient. Be understanding. Be forgiving. Be open and honest.

Working It Out Activity:

1. What compromises can you and your friends make?

2. Remind yourself about what you appreciate in your friend.

3. You and your friends can make friendship bracelets and exchange them. These can be a reminder or your friendship.

Gossip Smossip and Other Games We Girls Play

"If you do not have anything nice to say to someone or about someone, keep your mouth shut." ~ My Mother

At some point your friends are going to annoy you. Other girls are going to annoy you. You are going to get jealous because your best friend decides to hang out with another friend for a day.

How many times have you and a friend taken the above scenario and blown it way out of proportion? I have and I know many girls have. You have that one girl that always has a better story than you; that one girl who has an annoying laugh; that one girl who is always so competitive; or you feel like just because your friend decides to hang out with another friend for a day that you are no longer friends. Why are we girls so hard on each other?

First of all let us look at the quote I put at the beginning of this chapter: "If you do not have anything nice to say to someone or about someone, keep your mouth shut." I cannot tell you how many times I heard this from my mother. I would hear it in my sleep because she had said it so many times. But you know, those were some of the wisest words she ever gave me.

I have repeatedly said throughout this book that we are not perfect, nor is anyone perfect. Whatever may be bothering us about someone else is, guess what - OUR PROBLEM. We are the ones that are feeling the emotions, and they are OUR EMOTIONS TO DEAL WITH.

So how do you deal with these emotions?

1. First of all--STOP. Stop all talking. Stop all actions.

2. Think:

    •   What is it about this person that annoys me?

    •   What has this person done to upset me? (Do I even remember what upset me?)

    •   Is any of this going to matter tomorrow or 50 years from now?

3. Rather than focus on what you do not like about someone, focus on what you do like.

    •   What can you learn from them?

    •   What are their good qualities?

I promise that if you follow these three steps, it will make you feel a whole lot better and will help you to accomplish the goal of finding something nice to say.

There will always be people in life that you do not really like or want as your friends. However, you still need to respect them. That means saying nice things to them or about them to others. It also means your actions need to show respect. If you want to have and to keep your friends, be kind and always speak the truth.

Respecting Others Activity:

1. What does the Bible say about speaking the truth?

2. Pray for others that "annoy" you.

CHAPTER FOUR

Your Great Adventure

We all have a power to do amazing, incredible things.

On this great adventure we call life, you will have different people enter your life, some helpful some more challenging. You will also face beautiful, wonderful moments and times of heartache and obstacles.

On this adventure, the way is not always clear, and even the people that support us in our life cannot always help us find our way. We have to learn on our own how to do things. We have to learn that within each of us lies a strength that is special only to us and is unlike anyone else's strength. We also must learn that we have so much potential if we just use what we have.

We all have power to do amazing, incredible things.

Fear of failure or fear of what others will think or say may be holding you back. Whatever it is, push it all from your mind. God created you to be who you are. You are one of kind. He created within you gifts and talents to not only help yourself but to help others. This is YOUR life! The people in your life are there to help guide, support and love you. Rely on them to help you through your adventure, but also believe in yourself! If you have dreams that you want to see come true, be ready to work for them. There is no one or anything that can keep you from reaching your dreams except you.

Dream Activity:

1. What dreams do you have for your life?

2. What strengths do you have?

3. Whom can you go to for support?

I Wish I May,
I Wish I Might…

I think casting our wishes to stars in the night sky is a way of naming those dreams and goals- the things our hearts really desire!

Have you ever looked out from your bedroom window at the night sky or stood outside on a beautiful summer evening and looked up into the wide, brilliant sky? It is amazing seeing the different stars, seeing Venus and Mars burning so brightly and seeing the different constellations. There is something magical about looking up at the night sky.

There have been many times that I have stood in my back yard both as a little girl and as an adult looking up at the sky, finding the brightest star and making a wish on it. I don't know how many wishes I have made on Venus thinking it was just a bright star. The wishes always varied from fitting in at school, to some magical way for the things that I thought made me look ugly to just disappear, having a boyfriend, or having dreams for the future come true.

In life, girls have many dreams or goals, and I think casting our wishes to stars in the night sky is a way of naming those dreams and goals or the things our hearts really desire. So what do we do with the wishes once we have said them?

Here's a little exercise. Write down as many wishes or dreams as you can think of. Make sure the wishes or dreams are things that can actually come true. Beside each thing you listed, write down things you would have to do to make each of them happen. You have to be willing to work and not just sit and daydream. Maybe there is a career that you want someday. Ask a trusted adult in your life to help you research about that career, what schooling or training will you need, what exactly you would do in that career, where you would have to live to do that career, etc.

Your life is what you make of it. You can fill it with whatever you choose. That is where the people in your life come into play. Throughout life you will be making decisions. Some are easy, such as what you want for breakfast, but many decisions are difficult. Having people that you trust in your life can help you with decisions that you have to make. I know sometimes you would rather just get advice from your friends instead of your family, but, trust me, your family is usually the best source for information. For the most part, they have your best interest at heart. It is so crucial that you know your values and the things that you stand for so that you know which advice is best for you.

Make a list of people that you trust--REALLY TRUST. Be sure to include people at home, at school and in your community that you know you can go to. Read over all of these people. All of them care about you. They want to be there to celebrate your achievements and to help you with challenges or heartaches. Go to these people whenever you need to.

You alone are responsible for your life. You choose what to fill your life with. When you make a wish, your dreams can come true!

CHAPTER FIVE

Love

We as human beings thrive on love-
to be loved and to love.

Love. Wow... I don't think there is a topic more popular than love. We as human beings thrive off of love--to be loved and to love. Sometimes this can become confusing depending on the family we have or experiences throughout our life. I think it would help all of us to define love.

Think about the people in life that you know love you. Think about the people you love. When you think of these people, you cannot help but think about why you love them. You have grown to appreciate things about them. They have grown to appreciate things about you. But above all, you are learning to truly get to know the people in your life and learning how to care for them. This is love.

To love someone else, you first have to love yourself. At the very beginning of this book we talked about getting to know yourself, being satisfied with yourself, and realizing the special person that you are. Along with all of this you must also love yourself by understanding and caring for yourself. It is all tied together, and the sum of it all is you.

You may experience heartache when someone you love does not love you back when you experience failure or when you experience disappointments. I have been there with a broken heart, and even though at the time you feel that you could never love again or you are afraid to get out there and try something new, I promise…YOU CAN.

Look to the people in your life. Who truly loves you for who you are? Who truly cares for you? Sometimes it is surprising to learn of the people that love you. They are from the most unlikely places.

I went with a choir group to sing Christmas songs at a church. I received a phone call a couple of days later that an older woman would like to be a mentor to a little girl that performed that day. Even though she had never met the little girl, she loved her. She wanted to give her understanding and care. We got the mentor set up, and it has been, as the ending of fairy tales go, "Living Happily Ever After."

Finding Love Activity:

1. What does the Bible say about love?

2. Whom do you love?

3. What do you do to show love to others?

Love From a Hero

Love does not only come from a handsome prince. It comes from those people in our life that sometimes either we do not realize or that we take for granted.

We have all read or watched the movies about fairy tales with the princess falling in love with a handsome prince. The handsome prince is seen as the hero and therefore the princess is finding love through her hero. As little girls, we have pretended to be a princess that has a prince fall in love with her. We see in the stories how everything is perfect, and we want that as well. What always amazes me is that we do not see the everyday love that we receive from true life heroes.

At the end of the last chapter, I told you about a woman and a little girl and the relationship they have built. Guess what? This lady is the little girl's hero. And guess what else? She is giving love to this little girl.

Love does not only come from a handsome prince. It comes from those people in our life that sometimes either we do not realize or that we take for granted. Think about your parents, your siblings, other family members, your friends. Think about your teachers, counselors, principals. Think about the people at your church, your Girl Scout leader, your coach for your sports team. All of these people love you! They want to take the time to understand you but also to care for you.

As kids, it is always hard to fully understand what the adults and other kids in our lives actually do for us. Your parents, or whoever you live with, provide you with shelter, food, clothing, and try their hardest to give you that popular toy that everyone else has. What about the adults in your school? They do what they do because they genuinely care about kids. I promise you it is not for the money or the benefits. Your troop leader or your coach are not there for the money or to say, "Look what I'm doing." They do what they do because they love kids.

But just as you have these heroes in your life, you are also a hero to someone else. You may not even know it. You could be a hero to your parent, others in your family, your friends, adults at school and at extracurricular activities. However, the ones that I think are always so heartwarming are the ones you probably never notice around you. The shy, quiet girl in class that no one talks to, the elderly lady that you helped, that one girl that you invited to eat lunch with you or to play at recess with you. You are a hero to someone else, and, whether you know it or not, you are showing love to someone else by understanding them and caring for them.

Life is wonderful, especially when we receive love from someone else. However, the absolute, most awesome part of life is when we give love to someone else. What legacy do you want to leave behind? Whom are you being a hero to?

Hero Activity:

1. Who is your hero?

2. How can you be a hero to others?

3. Read about Esther in the Bible. How was she a hero? What good qualities did she possess?

CHAPTER SIX

Conclusion

Be proud of the wonderful, young lady you are.

We have just completed an adventure in this book of getting to know ourselves, learning about forgiveness, making and keeping friends, and dreaming about tomorrow. There are many books out there about each of these topics, and I encourage you to read as many of them as you can.

Throughout your life you will be faced with many decisions, and you must find ways of dealing with situations. Look to your support system to help you. Pray over situations and take time to really think about them. Most importantly, TRUST YOURSELF. You are the expert on you. You are the only one that knows you inside and out. Look to your parents or other trusted adults for guidance and advice and RE-

ALLY listen to what they have to say, even if it is hard to hear. I promise you, they only want what is best for you!

Take the time to be available and open. Do not judge anyone. Look for the best in everyone! Look for the best in you! Take those gifts and talents that you have been blessed with and share them with others--even if you do not know them. Invite the new girl to eat lunch with you. Invite the girl that sits out at recess by herself to play with you and your friends. Give time to your community and try to find ways to make it better.

Embrace all that God has created you to be. I ask the students that come to my office, "Does God ever make any mistakes?" The answer is No. My response is, "Then you are not a mistake. God knew earth needed a (student's name) that possesses (student's gifts/talents)." We all have a purpose in life. We are all needed. But most importantly, and what I really want you to take away from this book—WE ARE ALL EXTREMELY AND UNCONDITIONALLY LOVED! Take that love and give it to others. Remember that to love is to really understand and care for someone else.

There is a particular reason why I chose the picture on the cover of the book. My husband and I went to Cypress Gardens in South Carolina. We were riding through a marsh in a canoe and came up to these beautiful lily pads. I noticed this one bright, brilliant flower and had to snap a picture. The lily represents each, individual girl. We are all different and hold a special beauty that is all our own. We are each unique, possess different talents and gifts, and have our own style. Be proud of the wonderful young lady you are!

Notes

Chapter One: Beauty and Me

1. Song of Solomon 4:7. NIV

2. Matthew 6:28-34. NIV